ABUNDANT TRUTH INTERNATIONAL MINISTRIES

Abundant Truth Leadership Series

Troubled On Every Side

How God Uses People and Problems to Prepare Us for Ministry and Service

Roderick Levi Evans

Troubled On Every Side

How God Uses People and Problems to Prepare Us for Ministry and Service

All Rights Reserved © 2009 by Roderick L. Evans

No part of this book may be reproduced or transmitted in any form or by any means, graphic, electronic, or mechanical, including photocopying, recording, taping, or by information storage or retrieval system, without the permission in writing from the publisher.

Front & Back Cover Designs by Abundant Truth International Publishing
Image by Arnie Bragg from Pixabay

Abundant Truth Publishing
an imprint of Abundant Truth Publishing
For information address:
Abundant Truth International
P.O. Box 126
Camden, NC 27921

ISBN 13: 978-1-60141-527-1

Printed in the United States of America

Unless otherwise indicated, all of the scripture quotations are taken from the *Authorized King James Version* of the Bible. Scripture quotations marked with NIV are taken from the *New International Version* of the Bible. Scripture quotations marked with NASV are taken from the *New American Standard Version* of the Bible. Scripture quotations marked with Amplified are taken from the *Amplified Bible*.

Contents

Introduction

Chapter 1 – Persons & Personalities   1

Paul & Timothy   4
David & Saul   14

Chapter 2 – Trials, Tests, & Tribulations   29

The Terror of Men   36
The Temptations of the Flesh   40
The Trauma of Setbacks   48

Bibliography   55

Introduction

God anoints and endows individuals with gifts and talents to serve in the Church. However, some have missed the very purpose of gifts and ministries in the Church. In the Abundant Truth Leadership Series, we will endeavor to present a proper foundation for believers to minister upon.

In this publication

Time would fail to try to explain all of the dynamics that are associated with God's preparation process for ministry and service. There is a definite art to how He does it. The only person that can hinder us is ourselves. We just have to learn to navigate through the difficult times of preparation for ministry and service. Paul summed up his toils of ministry when he declared,

We are troubled on every side, yet not distressed; we are perplexed, but not in despair; Persecuted, but not forsaken; cast down, but not destroyed; Always bearing about in the body the dying of the Lord Jesus, that the life also of Jesus might be made manifest in our body. 2 Cor 4:8-10 (KJV)

It is evident that Paul embraced problematic people and situations as a part of ministry. If we will have and maintain effective ministry and service, we must adopt this mindset. Why? God, in His wisdom, uses unusual things to prepare His people for service.

In the third book of this series, we give a brief study in which we will discuss how God uses people and problems to prepare us before and during ministry for effective service.

TROUBLED ON EVERY SIDE

How God Uses People and Problems to Prepare Us for Ministry and Service

-Chapter 1-

Persons & Personalities

TROUBLED ON EVERY SIDE

How God Uses People and Problems to Prepare Us for Ministry and Service

Let's get right to it. Biblical history has shown that God uses man to fulfill His plan and purpose. After creation, He brought the animals to Adam in order for him to name them.

Before destroying the earth, He spoke to Noah to send warning. When the worship of God in the earth diminished, He called Abram.

The same holds true today. He gives men the privilege to minister and serve in His. However, God does not always name prepare us in a personal manner.

Though God can deal with us personally, He still uses people to help prepare us for ministry. In this section, we will look at two biblical examples of how God used people to help prepare His servants for service. ***

Paul and Timothy

In preparing us for ministry, God will send individuals in our lives for specific periods of time. We cannot take these things lightly.

He will send us mentors who will

directly influence our work in the Kingdom of God. They will act as spiritual fathers and mothers to help prepare us for ministry and service.

Paul alluded to this in his writings. He told the believers that they had many teachers, instructors, or guardians, but not fathers; that is, individuals who had a personal connection with them in terms of ministry.

You may have countless Christian guardians, but you don't have many {spiritual} fathers. 1 Cor 4:15 (GW)

There are numerous biblical examples of saints who were mentored by others before entering into ministry. The relationship between Paul and Timothy is a classic example of this. Through their relationship, we will discover how God uses people in our lives.

Then came he to Derbe and Lystra: and, behold, a certain disciple was there, named Timotheus, the son of a certain woman, which was a Jewess, and believed; but his father was a Greek: Which was well reported of by the brethren that were at Lystra and Iconium. Him would Paul have to go forth with him... (Acts 16:1-3)

Paul met Timothy early in his ministry. After leaving certain areas because of threats, Paul meets Timothy and decides to bring him along. ***If God plans for someone to mentor you, you do not have to go and look for***

them. They will find and choose you according to the will of God. Remember the story of Elijah and Elisha.

> *So he departed thence, and found Elisha the son of Shaphat, who was plowing with twelve yoke of oxen before him, and he with the twelfth: and Elijah passed by him, and cast his mantle upon him.*
> *1 Kings 19:19 (KJV)*

Elisha was plowing when Elijah came and threw his cloak on him. God knows who has what we need. We have to be careful not to try and pick who we want to mentor us.

This chapter is titled persons and personalities because the people He sends to help us will have the personality we need along with the spiritual insight to push us in the right direction.

Neglect not the gift that is in thee, which was given thee by prophecy, with the laying on of the hands of the presbytery. Meditate upon these things; give thyself wholly to them; that thy profiting may appear to all. Take heed unto thyself, and unto the doctrine; continue in them: for in doing this thou shalt both save thyself, and them that hear thee. (I Timothy 4:14-16)

We discover in a letter to Timothy, Paul exhorts him not to neglect his gift. When God places someone in your life, they will encourage you continually to fulfill the call of God that is on your life. We also find that Paul's concern goes beyond Timothy fulfilling a calling; it extended to his very salvation.

Those whom God place in your life will not only deal with your ministry, but also with your walk with God. Paul repeatedly gave Timothy warnings (even after he began ministering) concerning his personal walk.

For the love of money is the root of all evil: which while some coveted after, they have erred from the faith, and pierced themselves through with many sorrows. But thou, O man of God, flee these things; and follow after righteousness, godliness, faith, love, patience, meekness. (I Timothy 6:10- 11)

Pray and ask the Lord to give you mentors for your benefit. However, you must be prepared to receive the mentors that He sends. You have to be humble and receive those whom God gives you. **Remember, you may have different mentors at different times in your life.**

Oftentimes, your relationship will be more like instructor and student rather than "equals."

Sometimes this dynamic can be humbling. However, it is a part of God's process. Mentors will sometimes anger you, challenge you, rebuke you, encourage you, and push you. They are only fulfilling what God has called them to do.

If you desire effective ministry and service, you will endure the unfavorable dynamics of the relationship. Appreciate those whom God will send in your life. ***This is especially true concerning your pastors.*** They usually will be there as certain mentors come and go.***

David and Saul

Most of us are comfortable with God sending someone in our lives to tutor and train us through instruction and example as we prepare for ministry and service. However, God allows people in our lives that only irritate, challenge, annoy, and anger us.

These individuals appear to be of the enemy. But, God will even use them to prepare us for ministry. When He wanted to correct Israel, He would always use the surrounding nations to teach them to obey Him. Isaiah records,

For with stammering lips and another tongue will he speak to this people. (Isaiah 28:11)

God spoke to Isaiah and said that He would speak to Israel through foreigners. What did He mean? They would not come and tell Israel to return to God. But, as they attack and come against Israel, they would understand that God was speaking to them to return to Him.

We have people in our lives that stand before us consistently as enemies. However, their involvement in our lives keeps us before the Lord and allows us to see what is in us. The story of David and Saul illustrates this.

We know that Saul was Israel's first king. He continually disobeyed God and was rejected. David was chosen to take his place. Their initial meeting was good.

> *Wherefore Saul sent messengers unto Jesse, and said, Send me David thy son, which is with the sheep. And Jesse took an ass laden with bread, and a bottle of wine, and a kid, and sent them by David his son unto Saul. And David came to Saul, and stood before him: and he loved him greatly; and he became his armour-bearer. And*

Saul sent to Jesse, saying, Let David, I pray thee, stand before me; for he hath found favor in my sight. (I Samuel 16:19-22)

However, Saul turned against David later. The result was that David had to flee from Saul.

And Saul sought to smite David even to the wall with the javelin: but he slipped away out of Saul's presence, and he smote the javelin into the wall: and David fled, and escaped that night. Saul also sent messengers unto David's house, to watch him, and to slay him in the morning: and Michal David's wife told him, saying, If thou save not thy life to night, to morrow thou shalt be slain. So Michal let David down through a window: and he went, an fled, and escaped (I Samuel 19:10-12)

God could have killed Saul and placed David directly on the throne. Yet, the book of I Samuel gives account after account of David running from

Saul. God used the jealousy and anger of Saul to make David into a warrior. While fleeing from Saul, he gathered a following.

> *And every one that was in distress, and every one that was in debt, and every one that was discontented, gathered themselves unto him; and he became a captain over them: and there were with him about four hundred men. (I Samuel 22:2)*

From this, he learned how to be a

leader. Kings during that time were military leaders. He learned strategy in warfare from years of running from Saul. God allowed his enemy to test and try him. His story should encourage us.

Likewise, there are people in our lives who do not like us. We hate to see them coming. They, like Saul, throw javelins at us to try to kill us.

God is using those things to prepare us for ministry. It becomes your responsibility to discover what lessons these individuals are there to teach you. God can remove individuals from our lives in an instant. If He does not do this, we then must pray and ask God for understanding. His ways are not our ways.

For my thoughts are not your thoughts, neither are your ways my ways, saith the LORD. Isaiah 55:8 (KJV)

Here are three questions that one can present before the Lord in discerning the overall purpose for an individual being allowed to antagonize us.

1. Why doesn't this person like me?

God may want you to be delivered from feeling that everyone has to like you. That mentality has no place in ministry. We have to avoid ministering for the praise and acceptance of others.

Therefore, He will allow individuals to respond to us unfavorably so that our motives in ministry will remain pure.

2. Why is this person always talking about me?

It may be that you have not learned how to be rejected and ridiculed and still walk in love. Jesus said that the servant is no greater than the master.

They called Him the devil, the prince of devils, and accused Him of having a demon. If he had to endure such things, we will have to also.

3. Why does this person annoy me?

It may be that you think your way

is the only way. God may be teaching you tolerance and acceptance of others. Oftentimes, our problems with individuals stem from personal preferences and not because of ungodliness.

Therefore, God places people in our lives who are nothing like us to teach us how to accept others as He accepted us.

Only God can give you the insight you need to handle difficult people. Remember, God uses the foolish things to confound the wise (I Corinthians 1:27). He uses people and their varying personalities to get the best from us in ministry and service.

One more point – these dynamics of interaction do not stop once you begin ministry and service. They will be a featured part of your Christian walk and service.

TROUBLED ON EVERY SIDE
How God Uses People and Problems to Prepare Us for Ministry and Service

Notes:

_____

_____

_____

_____

_____

_____

_____

_____

TROUBLED ON EVERY SIDE

How God Uses People and Problems to Prepare Us for Ministry and Service

-Chapter 2-

Trials, Tests, & Tribulations

TROUBLED ON EVERY SIDE

How God Uses People and Problems to Prepare Us for Ministry and Service

TROUBLED ON EVERY SIDE

How God Uses People and Problems to Prepare Us for Ministry and Service

The Lord uses people; those who are for and against us, to help prepare us for ministry and service. In addition, He uses the irritations of trials and tests. The Lord allows us to be tested and tried in order to mature us in Him.

Trials and tests prepare us to face the difficulties that come with ministry and service. Peter said that the testing of our faith is valuable in the sight of God.

Wherein ye greatly rejoice, though now for a season, if need be, ye are in heaviness through manifold temptations: That the trial of your faith, being much more precious than of gold that perisheth, though it be tried with fire, might be found unto praise and honour and glory at the appearing of Jesus Christ. (I Peter 1:6-7)

James encouraged believers to rejoice in their trials because it will birth in them the fruit of patience. Patience would, in turn, bring about maturity and completeness. These are important traits for anyone who wants fruitful ministry and service.

> *My brethren, count it all joy when ye fall into divers temptations; Knowing this, that the trying of your faith worketh patience. But let patience have her perfect work, that ye may be perfect and entire, wanting nothing. (James 1:2-4)*

God tests His people while preparing them for service. We will look at examples from the Old and New

Testaments. This should encourage us as we are being prepared for His service.***

Trials of Joseph

Joseph experienced trials for 13 years before the Lord exalted him in Egypt. Every area of his integrity was put to the test. In Genesis, chapters 37 – 40 we read the complete account of his life.

God had given him dreams of how he would one day be in a position of authority.

However, the next years of his life did not seem to support the dreams. Your level of service in the Kingdom is directly proportionate to the number of trials you will endure. God does not place us in ministry to fail.

Therefore, He will allow us to be crushed, disappointed, hurt, etc., that He may use us for His glory. Joseph's story should inspire us to endure the terror of men, temptations of the flesh, and the trauma of setbacks.***

The Terror of Men

After God showed him his future, Joseph's life took a turn.

And he said unto them, Hear, I pray you, this dream which I have dreamed: For, Behold, we were binding sheaves in the field, and, lo, my sheaf arose, and also stood upright; and, behold, your sheaves stood round about, and made obeisance to my sheaf. And his brethren said to him, Shalt thou indeed reign over us? or shalt thou indeed have dominion over us? And they hated him yet the more for his dreams, and for his words. And he dreamed yet another dream, and told it his brethren, and said, Behold, I have dreamed a dream more; and, behold, the sun and the moon and the eleven stars made obeisance to me. (Genesis 37:6-9)

His own brothers threw him in a ditch and sold him into slavery. Joseph had to learn how to forgive.

There are many leaders who lack compassion and mercy. Joseph had to acquire these qualities before the Lord exalted Him. We find that at the reunion of him and his brothers, he had developed them.

> *But as for you, ye thought evil against me; but God meant it unto good, to bring to pass, as it is this day, to save much people alive. Now therefore fear ye not: I will nourish you, and your little ones. And he comforted them, and*

spake kindly unto them. (Genesis 50:20-21)

If God places you in high service, will you abuse your power? Will you put your foot on the necks of others? We do not know if Joseph would have. God used trials to make sure he did not. You cannot know either, except He reveals it to you.

However, God knows the end from beginning. Therefore, He will prepare us. If you cannot operate in love and forgiveness, you are not ready to operate in ministry effectively. ***

The Temptations of the Flesh

After being sold into slavery, Joseph became the property of Potiphar in Egypt. While there, the Lord blessed him and he had favor in Potiphar's sight. Potiphar placed all he had under Joseph's control. However, his wife lusted after Joseph.

And he left all that he had in Joseph's hand; and he knew not ought he had, save the bread which he did eat. And Joseph was a goodly person, and well favored. And it came to pass after these things, that his master's wife cast her eyes upon Joseph; and she said, Lie with me. (Genesis 39:6-7)

Joseph had to make a decision. Would he violate his master's trust and God standards? He had to be accountable to himself and God. No Hebrews were there to remind him of God's standards.

Joseph's character shined even

when he was alone. He had to overcome because of where God was taking him.

> *And it came to pass about this time, that Joseph went into the house to do his business; and there was none of the men of the house there within. And she caught him by his garment, saying, Lie with me: and he left his garment in her hand, and fled, and got him out. (Genesis 39:11-12)*

If he did not overcome this temptation, he would be overcome by it in the future. Can God trust you in ministry and service? Do you use your

position and title to please yourself?

Are you a person of integrity now? Search yourself. We find that Joseph passed this trial, even though it cost him. She lied to her husband about him.

And it came to pass, when his master heard the words of his wife, which she spake unto him, saying, After this manner did thy servant to me; that his wrath was kindled. And Joseph's master took him, and put him into the prison, a place where the king's prisoners were bound: and he was there in the prison. (Genesis 39:19-20)

Overcoming this temptation caused Joseph a major setback. He went from being a servant to being a prisoner. He now had to face the trauma of setbacks. ***

The Trauma of Setbacks

Have you ever felt like you take one step forward and two steps back? Imagine how Joseph felt. He did what was right and it got him put in prison.

Some of you, presently, feel this way. You tried to do it God's way, but there seems to be no results. Do not worry. You are closer to your destiny than before. We find that Joseph overcame this setback. He still served God and was blessed even in the prison.

And the keeper of the prison committed to Joseph' hand all the prisoners that were in the prison; and whatsoever they did there, he was the doer of it. The keeper of the prison looked not to anything that was under his hand; because the Lord was with him, and that which he did, the Lord made it to prosper. (Genesis 39:22-23)

We find that Joseph still prospered after an apparent setback. Setbacks are inevitable. However, the enemy's setbacks are normally God's set-ups.

Joseph was in place (in prison) to interpret the dream of the man who would introduce him to Pharaoh, who in turn, would be used of God to elevate Joseph to his divine destiny.

Sometimes what appears to be a setback is God's mode of elevation. He does this so that we will know that it is He that has called us and placed us in a particular area to serve.

This was the ultimate plan of the Father.***

The Tests of the Apostles

Briefly, we will look at how Jesus tested the apostles. They followed Him for three years. However, Jesus wanted to ensure that they would continue after He left. Ministry requires faith. Faith ca only grow if it is exercised, tested, and tried.

After Jesus taught them on the principles of holy living, He had to show them the blueprint for operating in the power of God. The tests were designed to push them further in ministry.

The Apostles at Sea

> And the same day, when the even was come, he saith unto them, Let us pass over unto the other side. And when they had sent away the multitude, they took him even as he was in the ship. And there were also with him other little ships. And there arose a great storm of wind, and the

waves beat into the ship, so that it was now full And he was in the hinder part of the ship, asleep on a pillow: and they awake him, and say unto him, Master, carest thou not that we perish? And he arose, and rebuked the wind, and said unto the sea, Peace, be still. And the wind ceased, and there was a great calm. And he said unto each them, Why are ye so fearful? how is it that ye have no faith? (Mark 4:35-40)

The gospels record this particular incident. We find that Jesus tested their faith because they had already seen Him perform many miracles. However, as soon as the storm came, they became afraid. We would think that they had a right to be afraid. But the scriptures record that Jesus rebuked them by asking them why don't you have any faith?

This account is one of many. If you wonder why you go through numerous situations, it is because God is building faith in you. This faith, in turn, will produce great results in ministry and service. He tested their faith in many areas, but the result of the faith was seen in their future ministries.

God allows us to experience lack` and to be placed in uncomfortable situations, that He may produce gifts and ministries in us that will impact the world.

TROUBLED ON EVERY SIDE

How God Uses People and Problems to Prepare Us for Ministry and Service

Notes:

_____

_____

_____

_____

_____

_____

_____

_____

TROUBLED ON EVERY SIDE

How God Uses People and Problems to Prepare Us for Ministry and Service

Bibliography

Smith, William. Smith's Bible Dictionary. Holman Bible Publishers. Nashville, Tennessee. c1994

The Bible Library. The Bible Library CD Rom Disc. Ellis Enterprises Incorporated, (c) 1988 – 2000. 4205 McAuley Blvd., Suite 385, Oklahoma City, OK 73120. All Rights Reserved.

Lockman Foundation. Comparative Study Bible. Zondervan Publishing House. Grand Rapids, MI, c1984

TROUBLED ON EVERY SIDE
How God Uses People and Problems to Prepare Us for Ministry and Service

Notes:

TROUBLED ON EVERY SIDE

How God Uses People and Problems to Prepare Us for Ministry and Service

_____

_____

_____

_____

_____

_____

_____

_____

_____

_____

TROUBLED ON EVERY SIDE

How God Uses People and Problems to Prepare Us for Ministry and Service

Notes:

TROUBLED ON EVERY SIDE

How God Uses People and Problems to Prepare Us for Ministry and Service

Notes:

TROUBLED ON EVERY SIDE
How God Uses People and Problems to Prepare Us for Ministry and Service

www.ingramcontent.com/pod-product-compliance
Lightning Source LLC
Chambersburg PA
CBHW050344010526
44119CB00049B/692